WHERE DID THE EARTH COME FROM?

Dr. Joshua Lawrence Patel Deutsch

In the beginning, nearly 14 billion years ago, all of the matter and energy in the universe existed in a small space, unimaginably dense and hot. Our universe may have begun no bigger than a person.

From that moment, the matter and energy spread apart in all directions. It expanded from the size of a person to an astronomical size in a fraction of a second. This was the birth of our universe, an event known as the Big Bang.

Scientists learned about the Big Bang by observing the stars. In the 1910's, astronomer Vesto Slipher noticed that most of the distant stars are racing away from us in all directions. By the 1920's, astronomer Edwin Hubble calculated that the more distant a star is, the faster it's moving away. These observations revealed that the universe is expanding. Moreover, by measuring the movement of stars backwards through time, it becomes clear that the further back we go, the stars get closer together. Scientists calculate that all matter originated in the same place around 14 billion years ago.

Edwin Hubble (1889-1953)

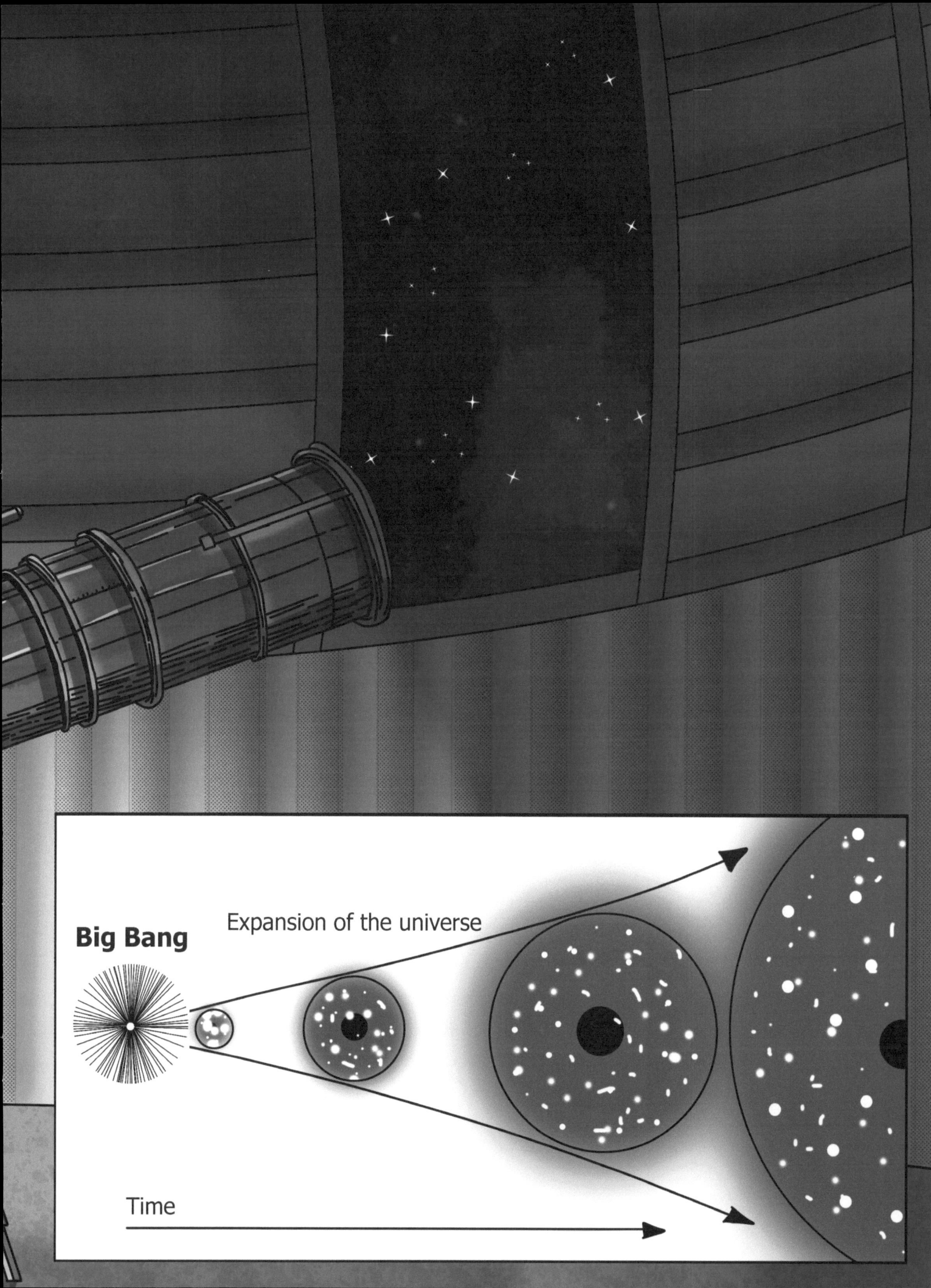

The Big Bang theory became widely accepted after 1965 when scientists with specialized telescopes detected energy waves from the Big Bang called cosmic microwave background radiation. These waves are evenly spread through outer space and match the expected characteristics for energy waves produced by the Big Bang.

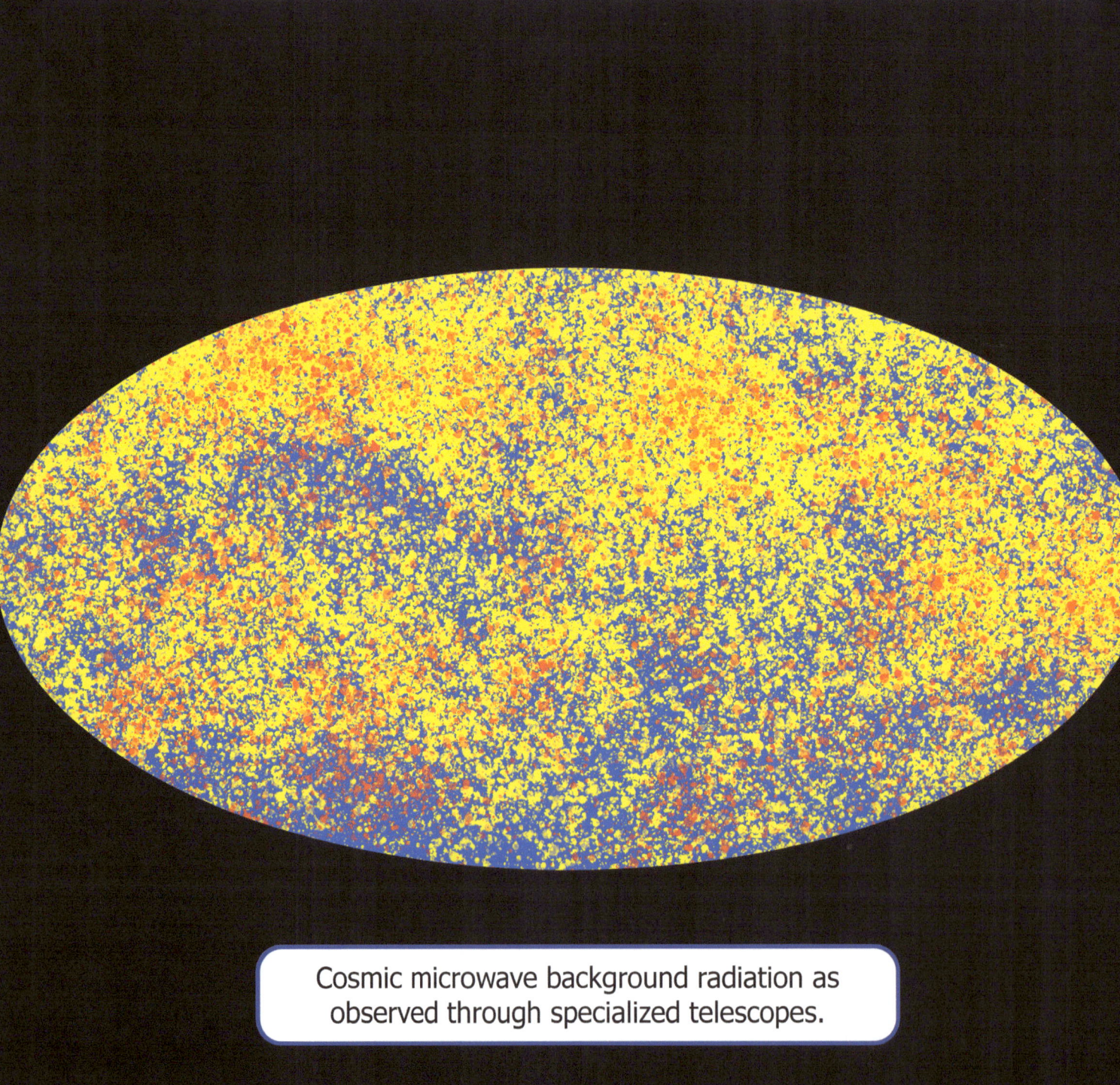

Cosmic microwave background radiation as observed through specialized telescopes.

After the Big Bang, most of the matter in the universe was invisible "dark matter." The rest of the matter makes up everything we can see. Within minutes, this ordinary matter formed into the cores of hydrogen and helium atoms, the smallest and most common of all atoms. These atoms clustered into giant clouds of gas, even as the universe continued to spread apart.

Atoms are the building blocks of ordinary matter. They are too small to be seen, but are detectable and measurable through scientific methods. If you break any object into tiny pieces, and keep breaking the pieces apart again and again, you end up with atoms. Atoms, in turn, are made from even tinier particles, which group together to form the 92 different types of atoms found in nature. Different combinations of atoms are responsible for the differences we see in ordinary objects. For example, water is different from concrete because the two substances are made from different combinations of atoms.

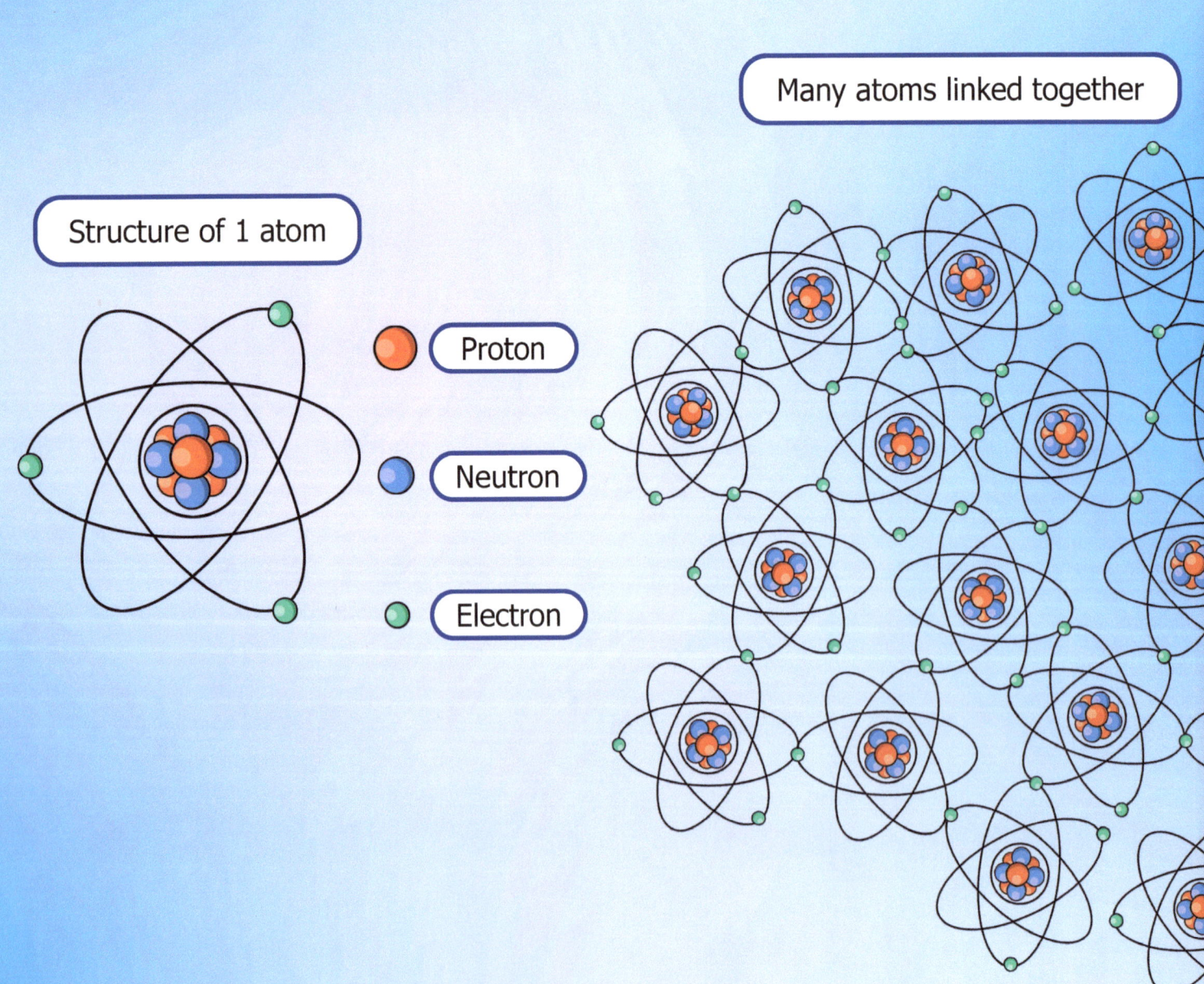

Matter has a force called gravity that pulls objects towards each other. The heavier the object, the more gravitational force it has. The Earth's gravity pulls you back to the ground when you jump. If the Earth did not have gravity, you could jump up to outer space!

Force of gravity

Due to the force of gravity, the gas clouds of hydrogen and helium atoms, formed after the Big Bang, condensed into stars and planets. Star and planet formation takes millions of years and new stars and planets continue to be born! Remember that most of the matter in the universe is invisible "dark matter," which also has gravity. Dark matter's gravity plays an important role in organizing the universe. In fact, we learned about dark matter by measuring gravity in excess of what ordinary matter could produce.

Star and planet formation

1. A giant cloud of gas and dust forms

2. Clumps begin to form within the cloud

3. The core of the emerging star becomes dense

4. The core condenses into a young star surrounded by a dusty disk

5. Planets form from the disk and a new solar system is born.

Due to its enormous mass, a star's gravity is so strong that the atoms in the center fuse together into bigger atoms. This process releases heat and light. Our sun is a star, just like many others in the night sky. The fusion of atoms in the center of the sun generates the heat and light that makes life on Earth possible. The temperature of the sun is 27 million degrees Fahrenheit (15 million degrees Celsius) in the center and ten thousand degrees Fahrenheit (5,500 degrees Celsius) at the surface. While many other stars are as powerful as our sun, none are close enough to Earth for us to feel their heat or see their light during the day.

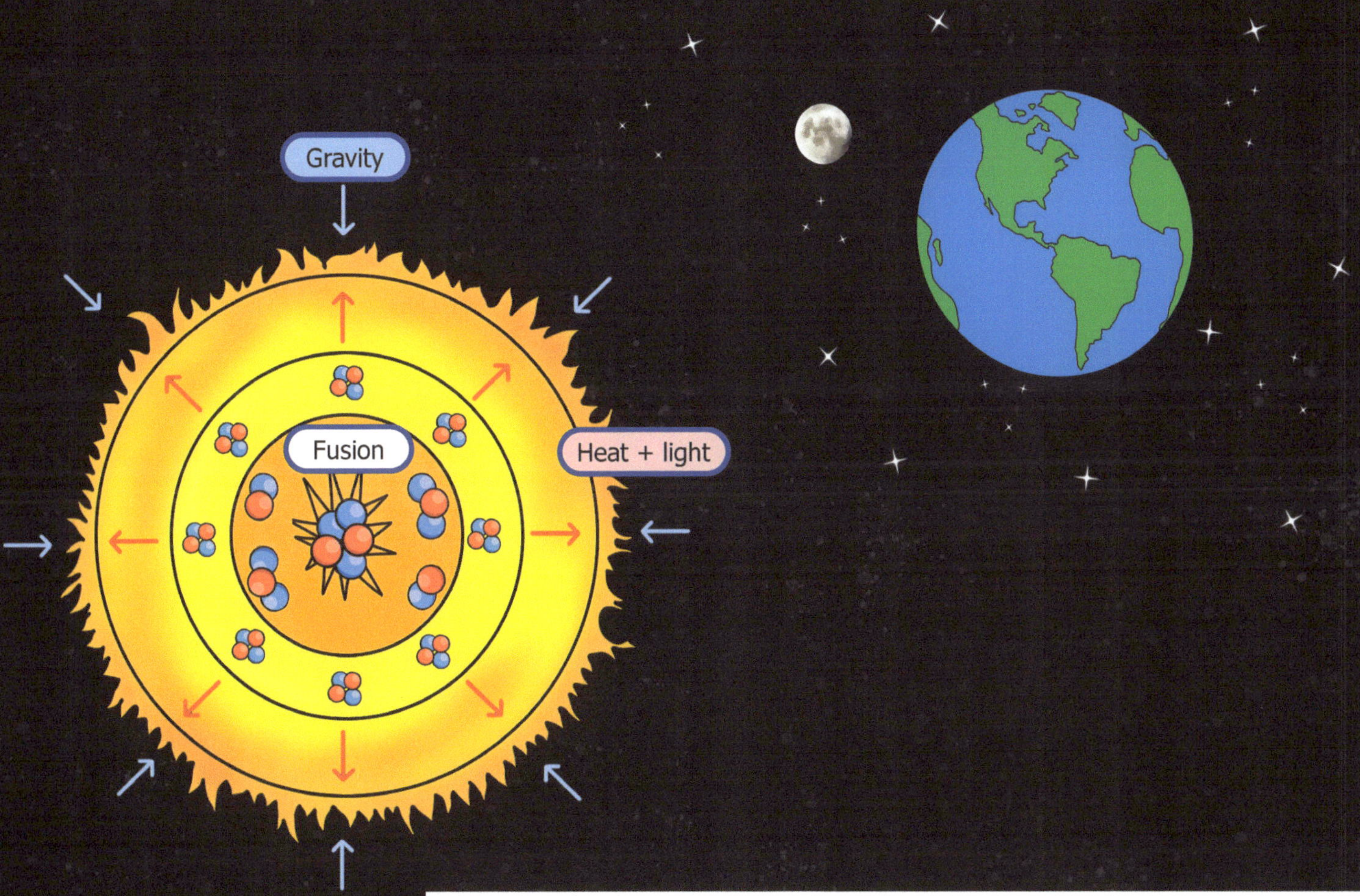

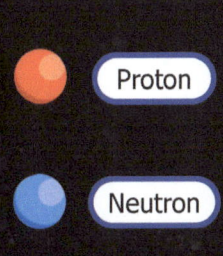

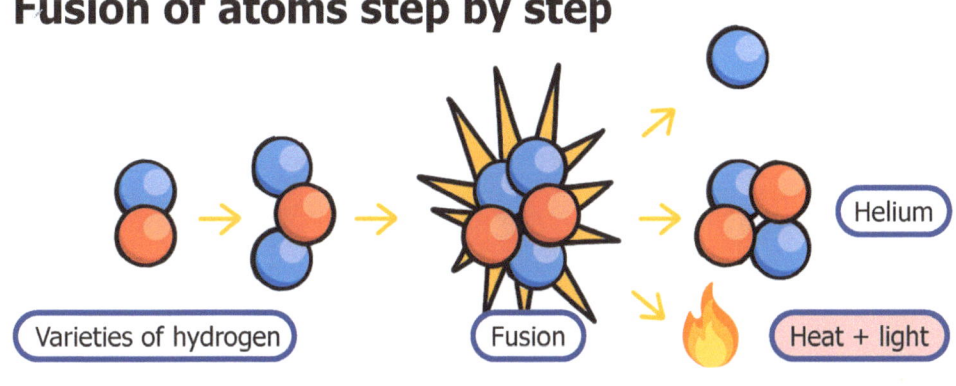

Fusion of atoms step by step

As hydrogen and helium atoms fuse together in the center of stars, they form bigger atoms like carbon, oxygen, nitrogen and iron. If a star explodes (supernova) at the end of its life, the bigger atoms are scattered and sent to other parts of the universe, where they can be incorporated into new stars or planets like our own. The Earth was fortunate to receive large quantities of the bigger atoms, which later became the building blocks of life.

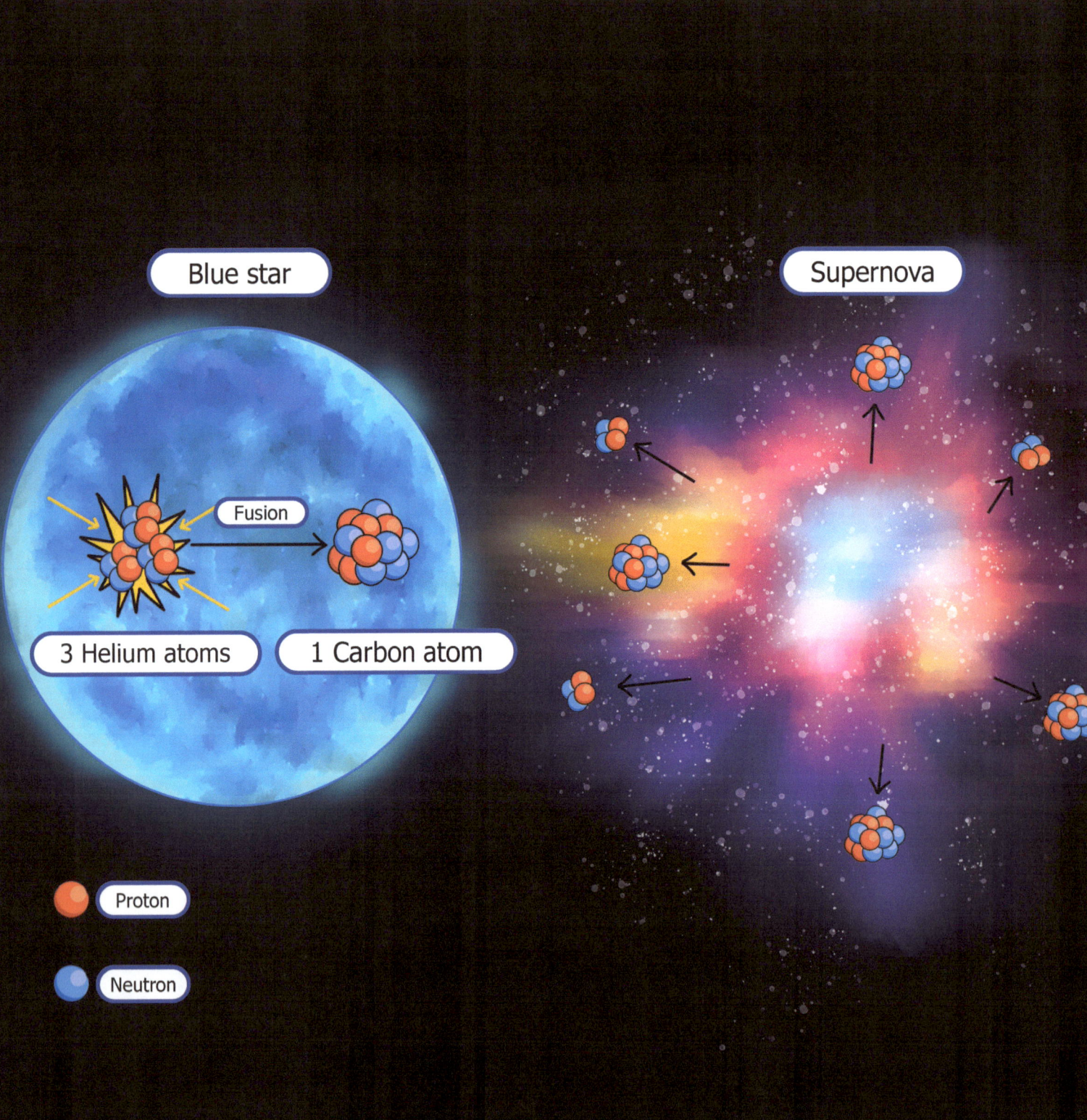

The Earth, and all life on Earth, is made from star dust. Our air is composed of oxygen and nitrogen. Water is made from oxygen and hydrogen. Plants and animals are built with carbon, and the genes of life contain carbon, oxygen and nitrogen. The iron in our blood carries oxygen throughout our bodies, which helps us turn food into energy. All of these bigger atoms were made in the center of stars that exploded long ago.

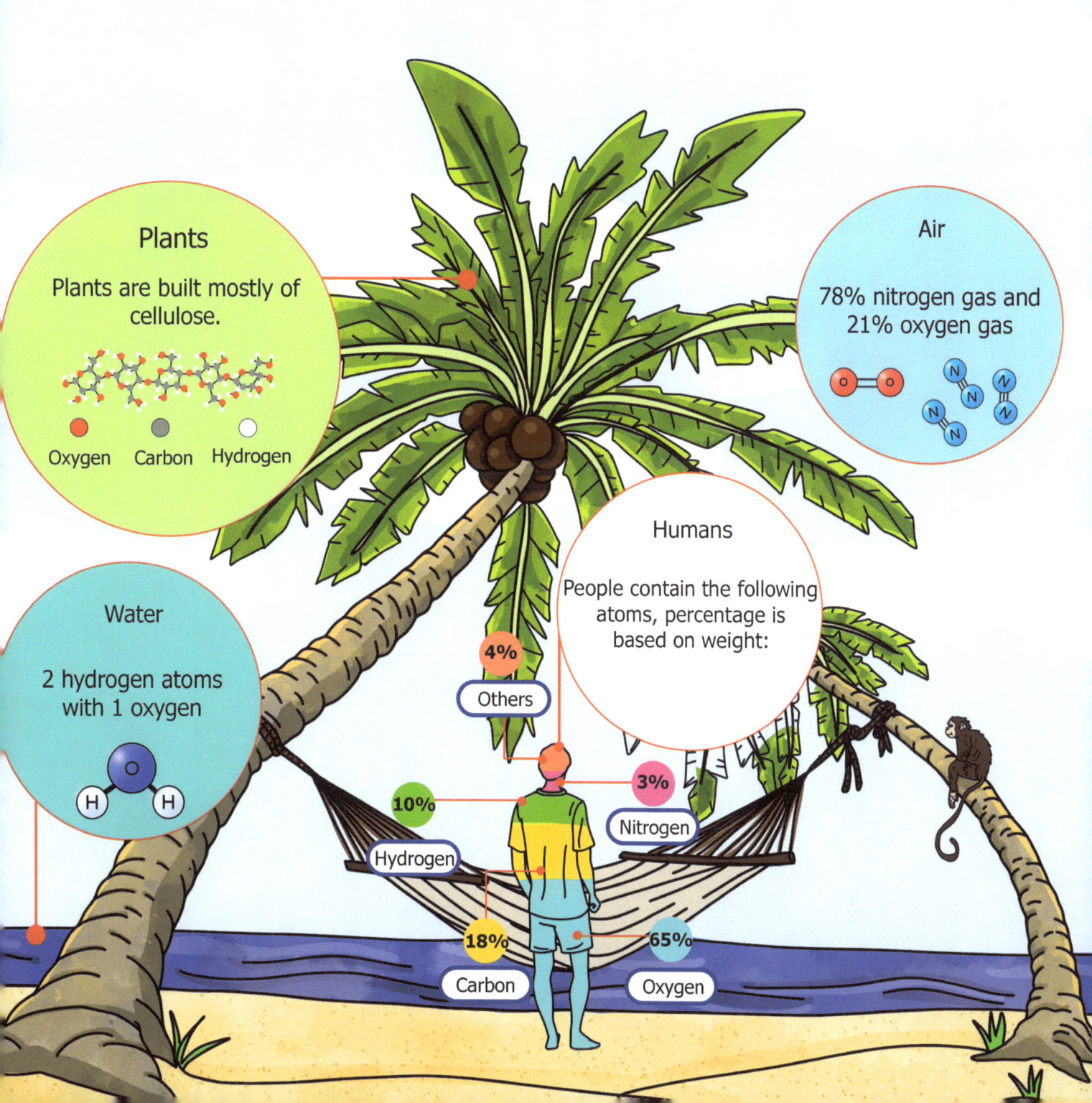

The Earth lives in a neighborhood of 8 planets that rotate around the sun. We call this neighborhood the solar system. The sun is bigger than a million Earths and 591 times as big as all eight planets combined. The sun's gravity holds the planets in circular orbit, like holding a ball by a string and spinning around in a circle. The distance between the sun and the Earth is 93 million miles (149 million kilometers). We are the third planet from the sun.

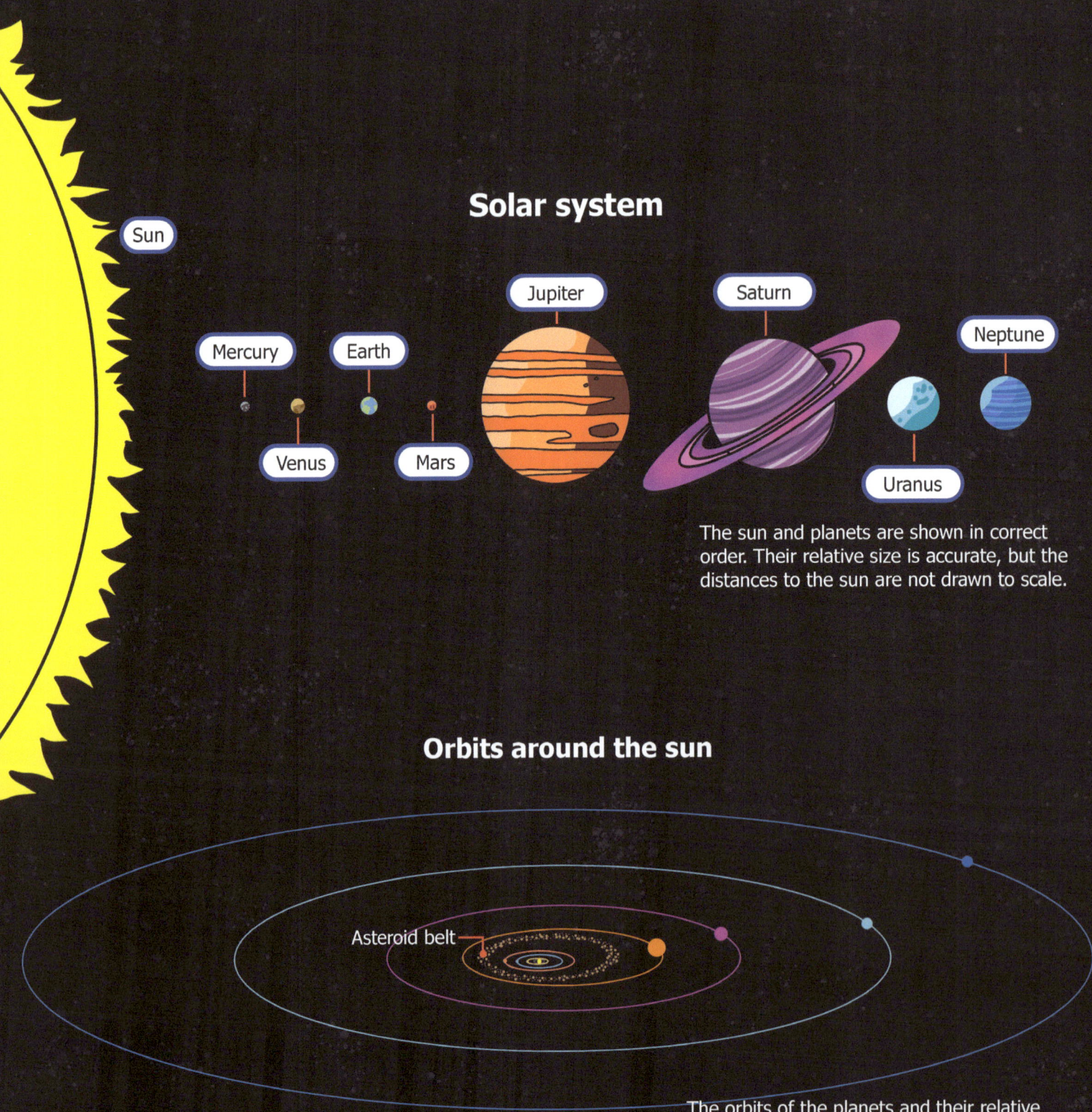

Solar system

The sun and planets are shown in correct order. Their relative size is accurate, but the distances to the sun are not drawn to scale.

Orbits around the sun

The orbits of the planets and their relative distances to the sun are drawn accurately.

Our solar system formed around 4.6 billion years ago from clouds of gas and rock. Some of this material came directly from the Big Bang, but most of it was recycled from exploded stars that released their gases back into outer space. The sun captured the majority of the gas cloud, and the planets, moons and asteroids captured most of the rest. The rotation of the planets around the sun is a continuation of the motion of the original gas cloud. Material moving at the wrong speed and direction either drifted off into space or crashed into the sun as the solar system was forming.

Formation of the solar system

A year is the time it takes for a planet to make a full circle around the sun. If you are five years old on Earth, you've traveled around the sun five times! However, Mercury, the closest planet to the sun, makes four revolutions around the sun before we finish one. So, the same five year old from Earth living on Mercury would be twenty Mercury years old!

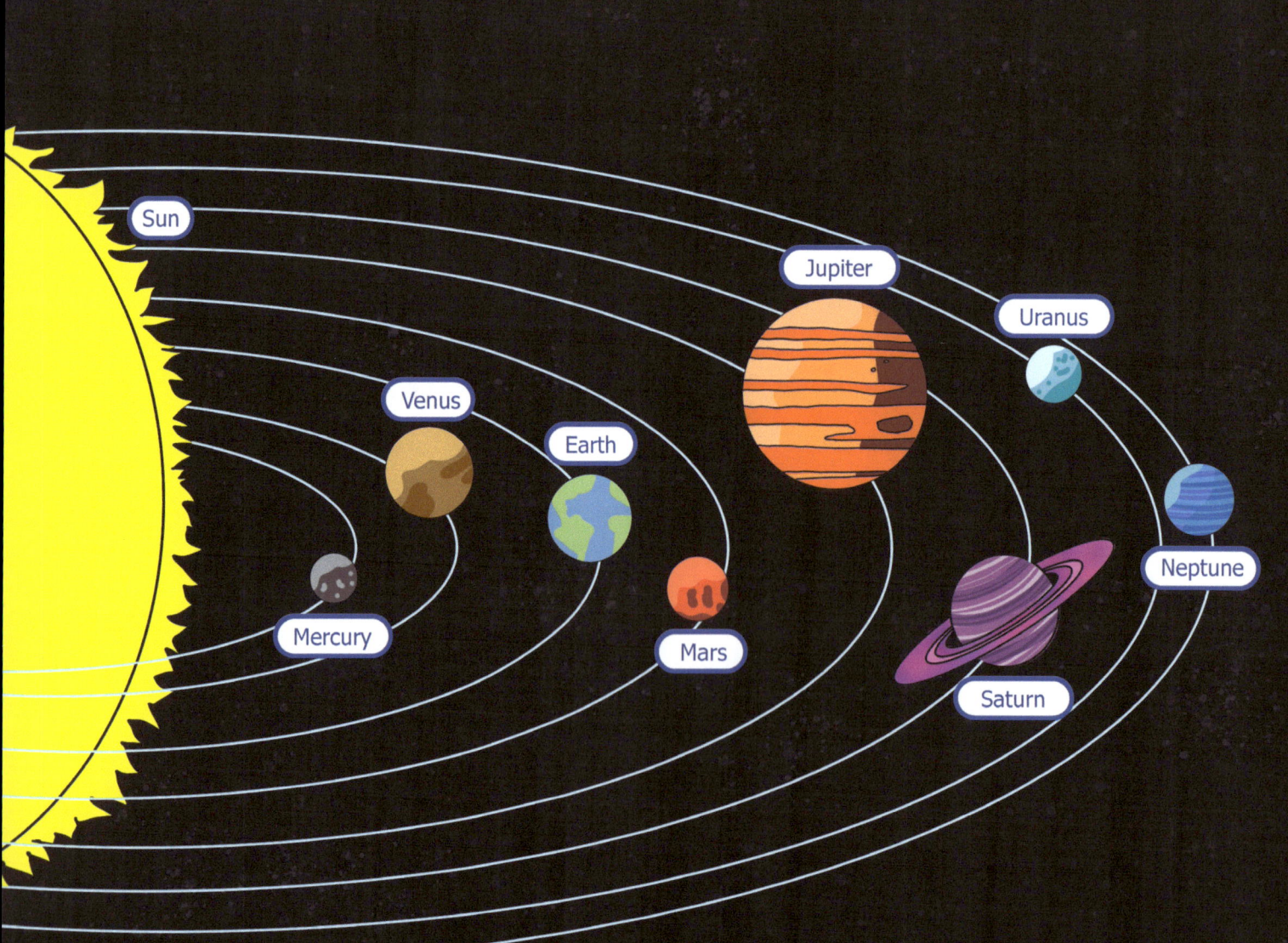

Planet	1 orbit	Earth time
Mercury	1 Mercury year equals...	88 Earth days
Venus	1 Venus year equals...	225 Earth days
Earth	1 Earth year equals...	365 Earth days
Mars	1 Mars year equals...	687 Earth days
Jupiter	1 Jupiter year equals...	12 Earth years
Saturn	1 Saturn year equals...	30 Earth years
Uranus	1 Uranus year equals...	84 Earth years
Neptune	1 Neptune year equals...	165 Earth years

The Earth's tilt in relation to the sun causes the change in seasons. During part of the Earth's rotation around the sun, we tilt towards the sun, and we experience summer. When we're tilted away from the sun, we get winter. Keep in mind that when the North tilts towards the sun, the South tilts away. Consequently, when it's winter in the North, it's summer in the South. Near the equator, the Earth hardly tilts, so there's much less seasonal variation.

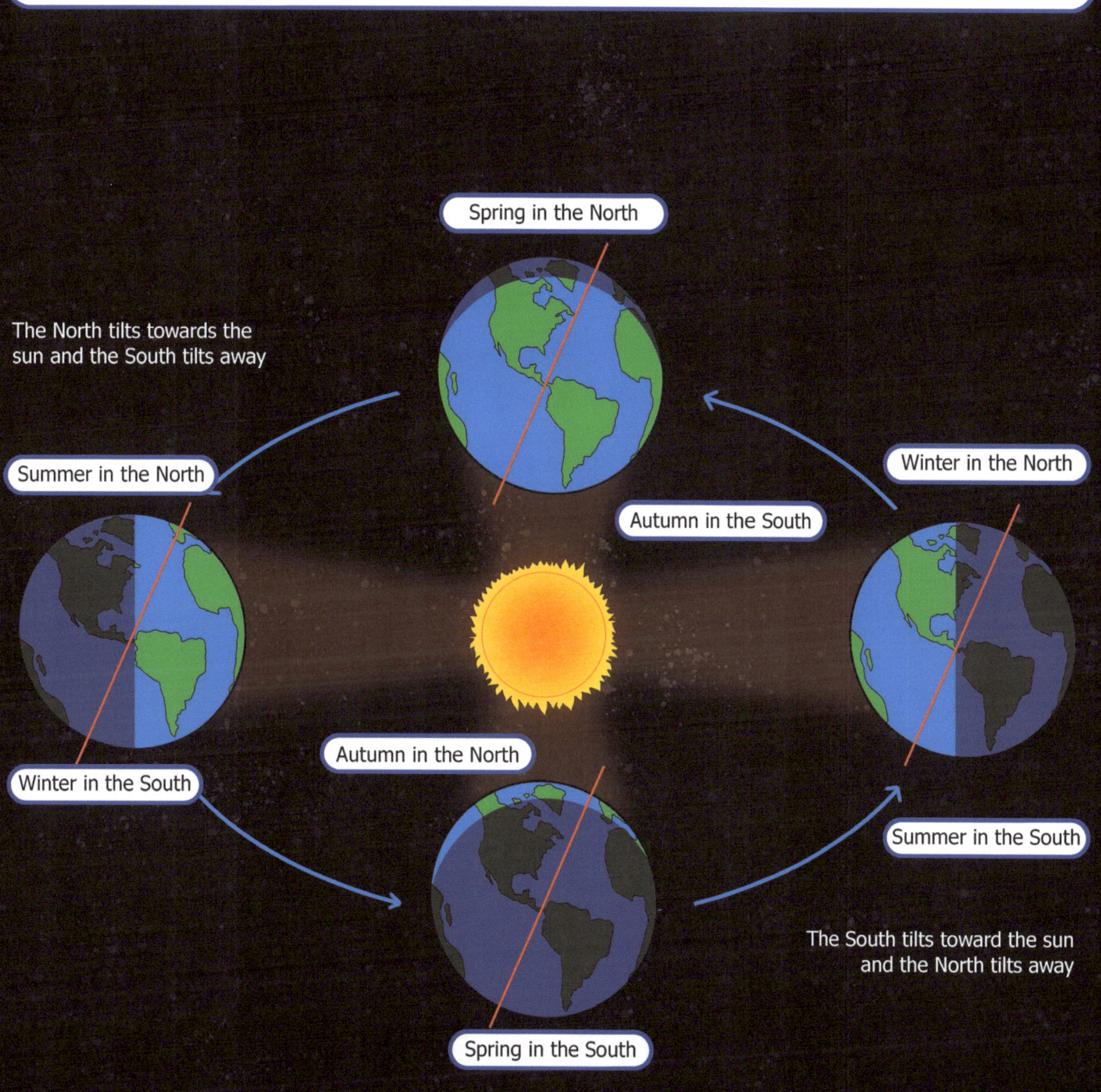

As the Earth travels around the sun, it also spins like a basketball on a player's finger. The Earth's spin causes daytime and nighttime. Daytime occurs when our part of the Earth faces the sun. When we face away from the sun, it becomes night. Keep in mind that when it's daytime for you, it's nighttime halfway around the world. Furthermore, the day's length is different on every planet. While Earth has a 24 hour day, Mars has a 25 hour day, and—on slow spinning Venus— a day lasts 5,832 hours!

The Earth races around the sun at a speed of 67,000 miles (107,000 kilometers) per hour. Simultaneously, it spins like a basketball at 1,000 miles (1,600 kilomiters) per hour at the equator. We cannot feel these movements, because everything around us moves at the same speed. Similarly, you can ride in a speeding car and feel like you're not moving. Wherever we go on Earth, gravity keeps us, and everything around us, connected to the Earth's surface. For most of human history, people assumed that the Earth was flat and the sun rotated around the Earth. It's natural for us to assume that things are as we perceive them. However, science often discovers that our perceptions are very different from reality.

Sunset from Earth

Sunset from space

Moons orbit planets in the same way that planets orbit stars. As a moon travels through space, its planet's gravity pulls it into circular motion. The Earth has one moon, a quarter of the size of the Earth, that brings light and beauty to the night sky. Mercury and Venus have no moons, Mars has two small moons, and Saturn has 146 in total. Planets acquire their moons in four different ways. First, some moons formed alongside their planets from the original gas cloud during the birth of the solar system. Second, moons can form when pieces of a planet break off during formation. Third, planets can capture moons when asteroids (small planets orbiting the sun) get pulled into the planet's orbit. Finally, collisions between planets, or between a planet and an asteroid, can cause fragmentation, with the ejected material becoming a moon.

Most scientists believe that the Earth's moon resulted from a collision. According to this theory, around 4.5 billion years ago, shortly after the Earth's formation, the Earth crashed with a planet called Theia. Theia was half the size of the Earth and traveled too close to the Earth's orbit. Theia fragmented during the collision, with some of it merging into the Earth, and some of it mixing with debris from the Earth to form the moon. Evidence for this theory comes from lunar soil and rock samples collected by humans who traveled to the moon on rocketships between 1969 and 1972. The moon's differences from the Earth suggest that they didn't form together, but the moon also contains material that likely came from the Earth. A collision between the Earth and another planet is the most likely explanation, and computer simulations show how this collision may have occurred.

Theia

Earth before the oceans formed

The moon's "light" is actually sunlight reflecting off the moon's surface. The moon has no light of its own. Although the sun always shines on half of the moon's surface, the amount of "moonlight" we see changes nightly as the moon orbits the Earth, making it seem like the moon is changing its shape. When no moon is visible, it's called a "new moon," and when the moon appears as a complete circle, it's called a "full moon." The full cycle from new moon to new moon–or from full moon to full moon–takes 29.5 days, corresponding to the time it takes the moon to orbit once around the Earth. The predictability of the moon cycle has been useful to human societies for creating calendars and measuring time. Although most societies now use calendars based on the sun, many holidays are still scheduled using lunar calendars, and a month is roughly the timing of one moon cycle.

The phases of the moon

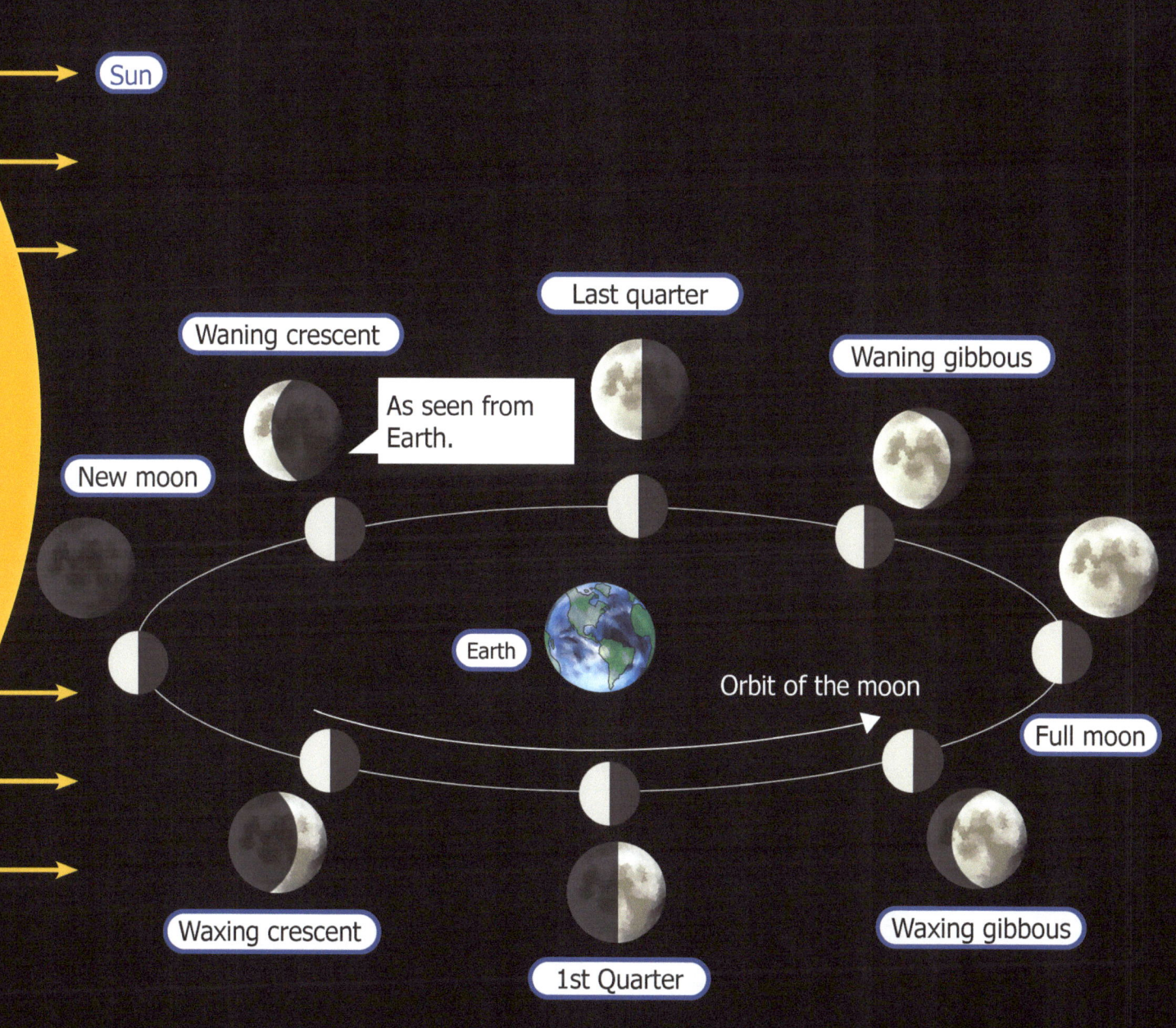

Life on Earth began in the oceans 3.8 billion years ago. The earliest life forms were small and simple like bacteria, but ultimately, they evolved into the complex organisms we see today. The Earth has two major advantages that facilitate life. First, we inherited bigger atoms like carbon, oxygen, nitrogen and iron that serve as the building blocks of life. Without oxygen there could be no water, and life on Earth needs water to survive. Secondly, our distance from the sun gives us a moderate climate. By comparison, Venus, which is closer to the sun, has an average temperature of 470 degrees Celsius, so water would instantly turn into steam. Mars, which is further from the sun, has an average temperature of -63 degrees Celsius, so surface water would freeze and become ice. It is much harder for life to exist in these extreme conditions.

Venus

Mars

Earth

Scientists believe that the very first life form arose by chance. In the early Earth's oceans, the building block atoms could mix like ingredients in a soup until they formed RNA, a configuration of atoms that can copy itself. Once established, these RNAs could interact to create better life-sustaining structures, with improvements occurring over time. The spontaneous creation of life likely occurred only once, with subsequent life evolving from earlier life forms. All life on Earth still uses RNA, which copies genes (inborn traits acquired from parents) and passes information from those genes to the rest of the body.

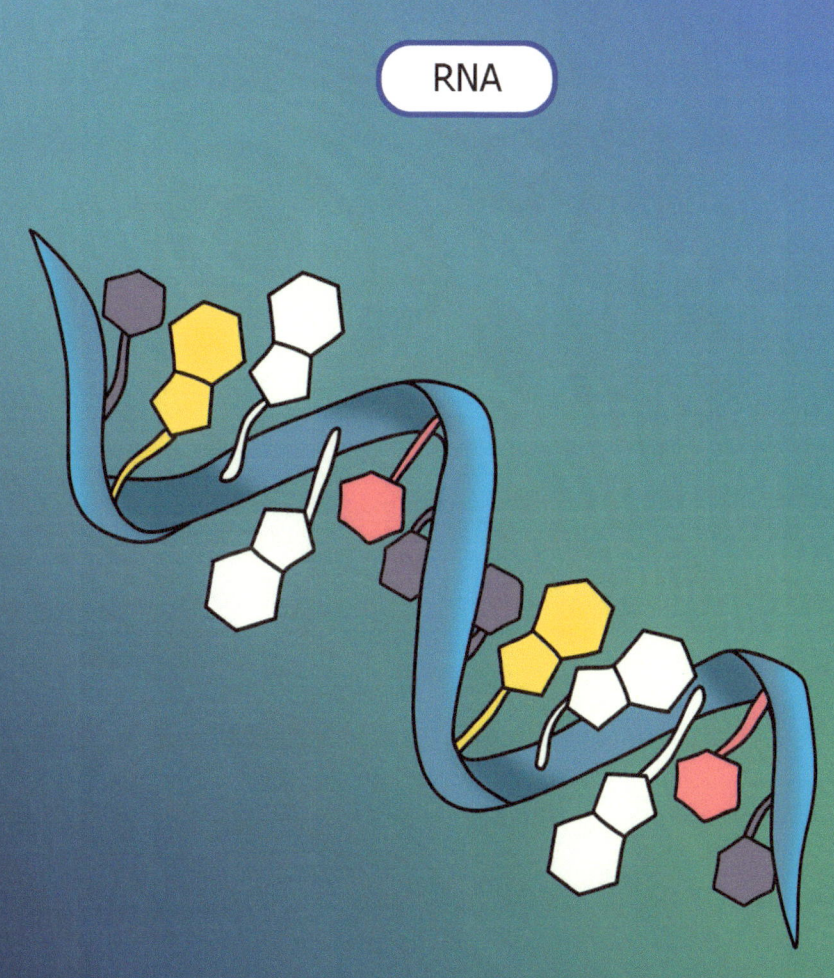

RNA

Life is rare and special. On Earth, we are blessed to have an incredible diversity of advanced and intelligent life forms. Humans, moreover, are both intelligent and technological, which makes us capable of exploring the mysteries of our universe. At present, we are not aware of life on any other planet except our own. However, given the size of the universe, with billions of trillions of planets, there must be more Earth-like planets where life as we know it could evolve. Furthermore, there may be alternative pathways for creating and sustaining life on planets different from our own. Such examples, if discovered, could change our understanding of what life is and how much of it is out there.

Should we go looking for life on other planets? Certainly, the discovery of life on other worlds would deepen our understanding of our place in the universe. Potentially, other worlds might have knowledge or resources that are useful to us. However, the meeting of two worlds could also be dangerous. The other world could be far more primitive or far more advanced than our own. One world might attempt to take over the other, or might accidentally transmit disease. Technological civilizations like our own, capable of exploring space, are also capable of incredible destruction. These civilizations may not survive past a certain point without embracing peace and environmental sustainability. By this logic, there is hope that an advanced alien civilization might choose to befriend us, rather than destroy us. By the same token, we ought to embrace peace in our own world before we go looking for others.

The universe is still expanding so fast that distant stars move away from us faster than light. This may seem impossible, since there are laws of physics that nothing can travel faster than light. However, the universe is not traveling in the traditional sense. The stars and planets themselves don't move even close to the speed of light. Instead, space within the universe is stretching, swelling or inflating like a balloon. The speed at which objects are spreading apart, as space inflates, is proportional to their distance of separation. So while distant stars are moving apart faster than light, the stars closest to us are hardly separating, and can even move closer together! The estimated size of the observable universe is 94 billion light years across. This means that if you could freeze the expansion of the universe and shine a light from one side, it would reach the other side in 94 billion years. By comparison, the sun's light reaches the Earth in eight minutes and twenty seconds. Since the universe, in reality, continues to expand faster than light, escaping the boundaries of our observable universe is impossible.

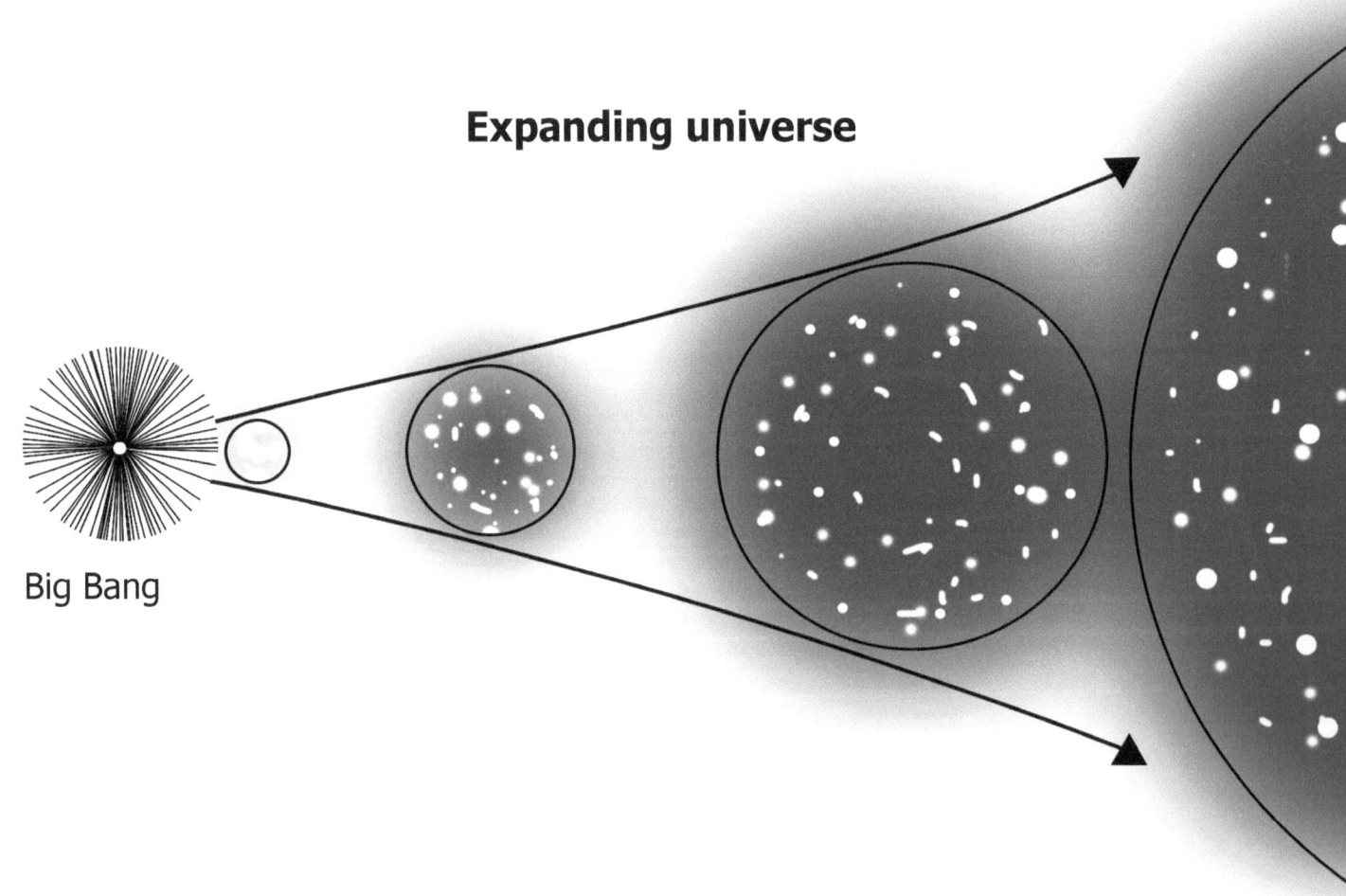

Expanding universe

Big Bang

Why is the universe still expanding? Not only is it still expanding, it's expanding faster over time! With the Big Bang over, gravity, in theory, should slow the expansion and could even shrink the universe inwards on itself. Matter would come back together again, recreating the original conditions before the Big Bang. But this is not what is happening. Scientists speculate that there must be a mysterious force called "dark energy" that opposes gravity and pushes the universe outward. The force of dark energy stays the same, whereas the effects of gravity get weaker as the universe spreads apart. Consequently, based on the current model, scientists predict that the universe will expand forever, and the rate of expansion will only increase.

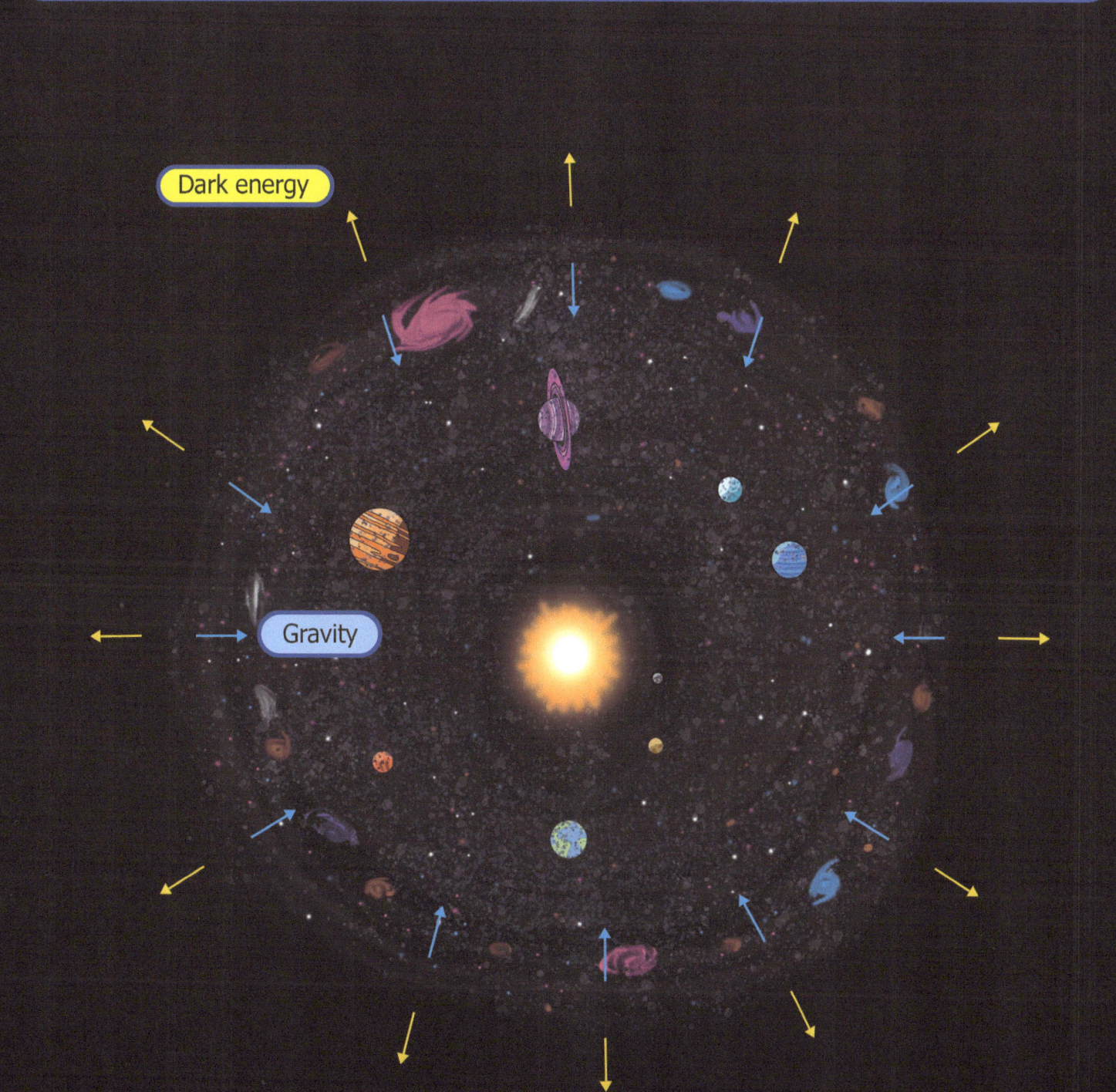

The Big Bang was the birth of our universe, but many mysteries still remain. What caused the Big Bang? What happened before the Big Bang? Scientists believe that a period called "cosmic inflation" preceded the big bang, in which our tiny, emergent universe, fueled by a massive burst of energy, expanded faster than the speed of light. Cosmic inflation may have lasted only a fraction of a second, and we don't know where the burst of energy came from. Nonetheless, scientists think that the inflation, and the burst of energy that caused it, gave rise to space, time, light, matter, and the laws of physics that govern our universe. Moreover, inflation sets the stage for the Big Bang, and the nearly 14 billion years that follow. The burst of energy, however, only adds mystery to our universe. Our observable universe is likely one part of a larger, unobservable reality. Additionally, there may be other distinct universes apart from our own. While our understanding of the observable universe has grown immensely over the past century, we can only speculate as to how the outside universe operates.

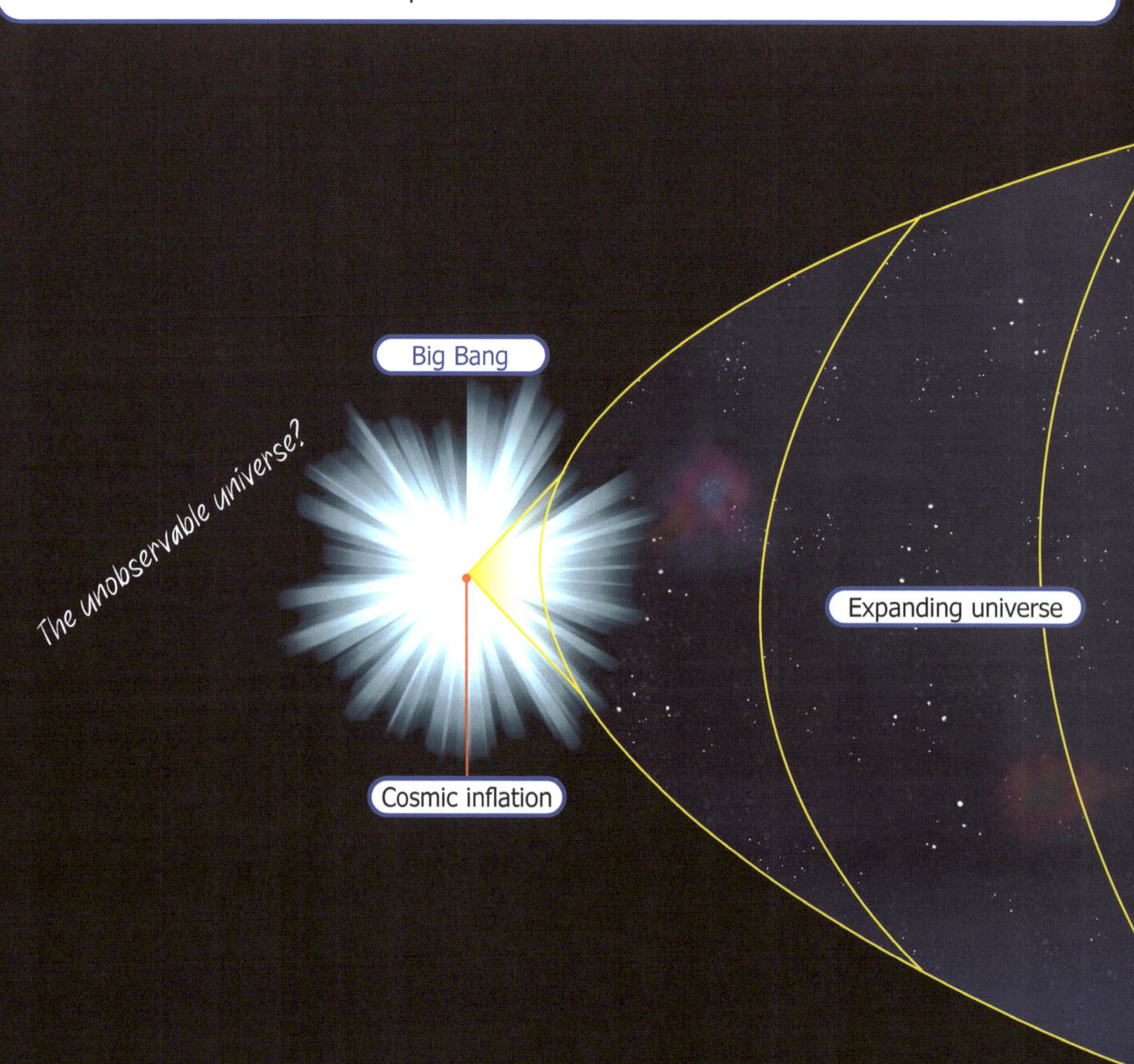

These are some of the remaining mysteries that scientists are still trying to figure out. We may never have the answers to some of these questions, but science is about the quest for knowledge. In only the last hundred years, our discovery of the Big Bang, and the formation of stars and planets, already provides fascinating insights into our past. We are just one species, living on one planet, orbiting one of 200 billion trillion stars in the vastness of outer space. Our universe may feel lonely, but it could be brimming with life, and there might be other universes out there, too. Still, as far as we know, we are the only species actively exploring the mysteries of our own creation. While these investigations may never reveal the reason for our existence, the search itself will hopefully empower us to discover our own meaning and purpose.

Other books by this author

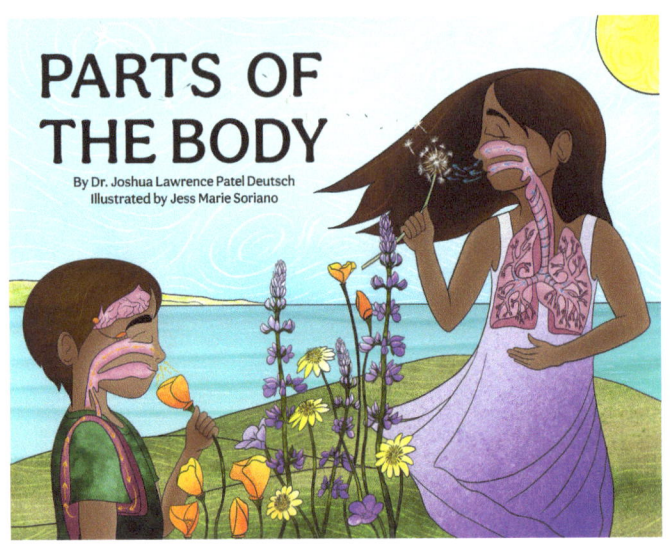

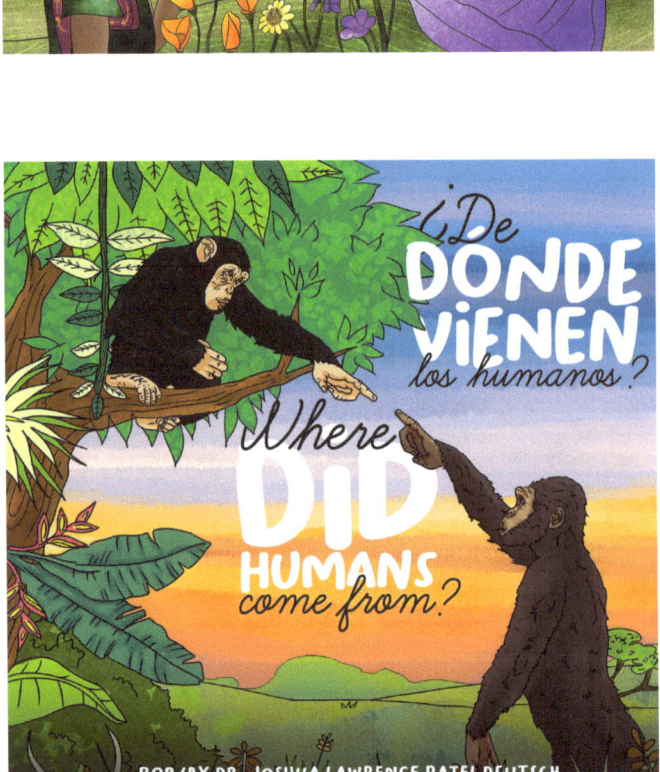

www.ingramcontent.com/pod-product-compliance
Lightning Source LLC
LaVergne TN
LVHW071659060526
838201LV00037B/387